Christmas Classics for Piano Duet

10 Seasonal Favorites for Two

ARRANGED BY ERIC BAUMGARTNER

ISBN 978-1-70514-145-8

WILLIS MUSIC

EXCLUSIVELY DISTRIBUTED BY

HAL•LEONARD®

Visit Hal Leonard Online at
www.halleonard.com

Contact us:
Hal Leonard
7777 West Bluemound Road
Milwaukee, WI 53213
Email: info@halleonard.com

In Europe, contact:
Hal Leonard Europe Limited
42 Wigmore Street
Marylebone, London, W1U 2RN
Email: info@halleonardeurope.com

In Australia, contact:
Hal Leonard Australia Pty. Ltd.
4 Lentara Court
Cheltenham, Victoria, 3192 Australia
Email: info@halleonard.com.au

From the Arranger

'Tis the season! This collection contains ten of the most beloved Christmas titles, all newly arranged for piano duet. I've strived to include a variety of moods and styles. As a result you'll discover some pieces lean towards the traditional while others offer up a fresh musical interpretation. I hope you get as much enjoyment out of playing these arrangements as I had in creating them!

Eric Baumgartner

Eric Baumgartner received jazz degrees from Berklee College of Music and DePaul University. He is the author and creator of Jazz Piano Basics, a series that presents jazz fundamentals in an accessible manner through short dynamic exercises. Eric is a sought-after clinician/lecturer who has presented throughout the US, Canada, England, Germany, and Australia. Currently he lives in Atlanta, Georgia where he maintains an active schedule as performer, composer, and dedicated member of the local music scene.

Contents

Ave Maria

Franz Schubert
Arranged by Eric Baumgartner

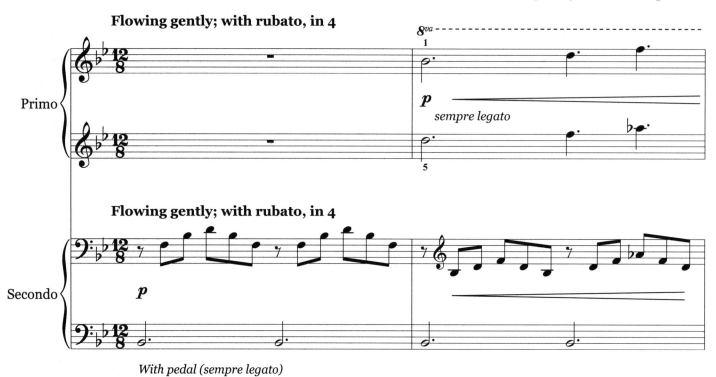

Bring a Torch, Jeannette, Isabella

17th Century French Carol
Arranged by Eric Baumgartner

Deck the Hall

Traditional Welsh Carol
Arranged by Eric Baumgartner

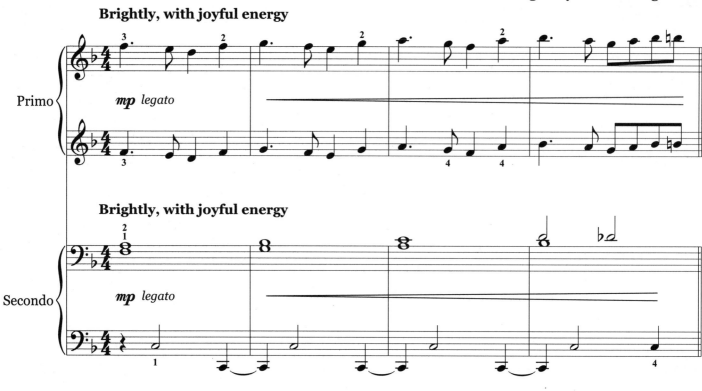

Here We Come A-Caroling

Traditional
Arranged by Eric Baumgartner

God Rest Ye Merry, Gentlemen

Traditional English Carol
Arranged by Eric Baumgartner

March of the Toys

from BABES IN TOYLAND

Victor Herbert
Arranged by Eric Baumgartner

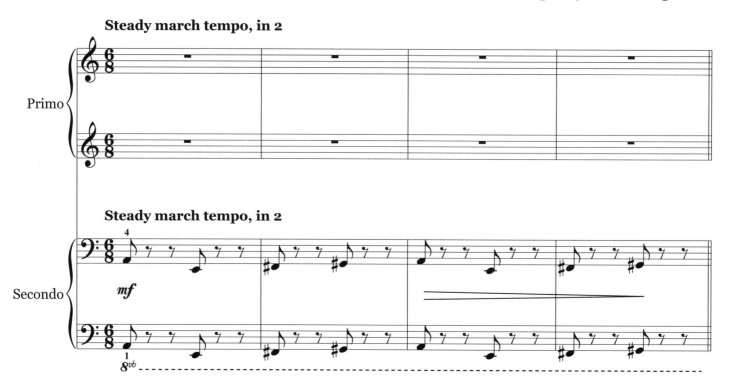

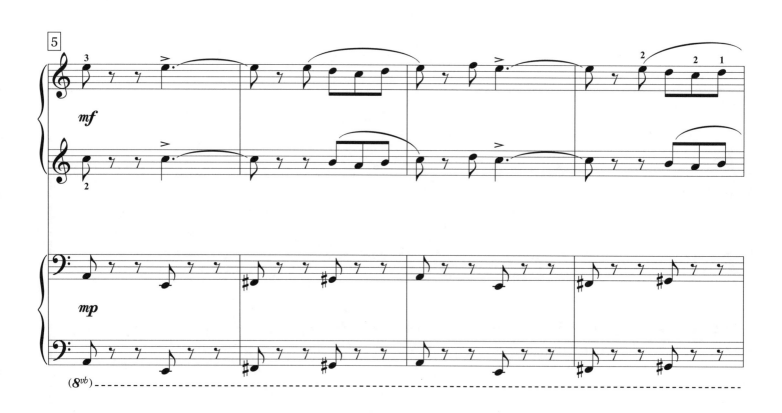

Waltz of the Flowers

Pyotr Il'yich Tchaikovsky
Arranged by Eric Baumgartner

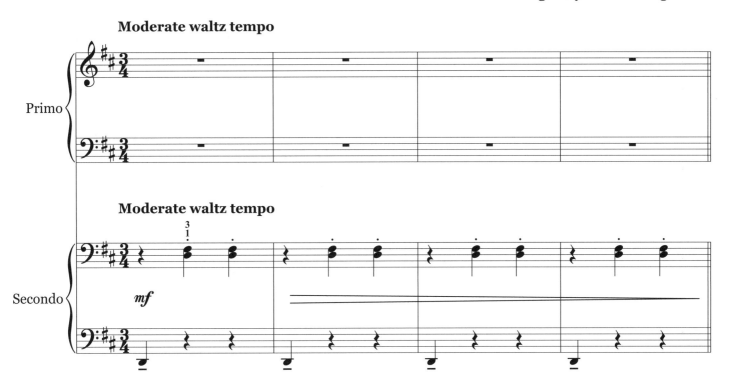

Silent Night

Music by Franz X. Gruber
Arranged by Eric Baumgartner

We Three Kings of Orient Are

John H. Hopkins, Jr.
Arranged by Eric Baumgartner

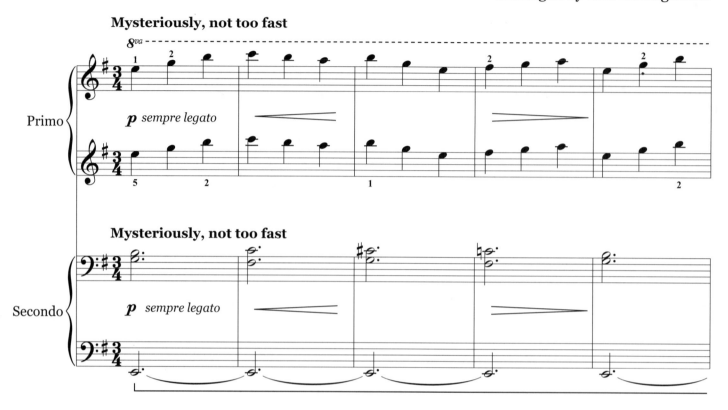

What Child Is This?

16th Century English Melody
Arranged by Eric Baumgartner

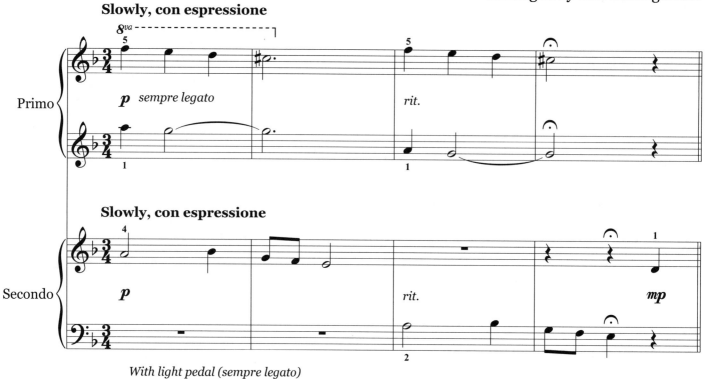

Other Christmas Collections
by Eric Baumgartner

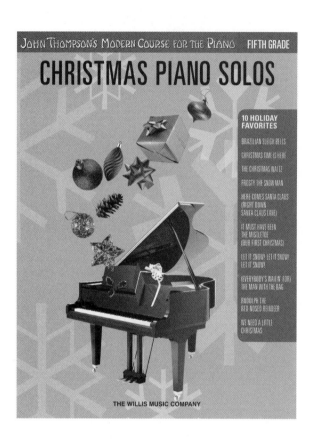

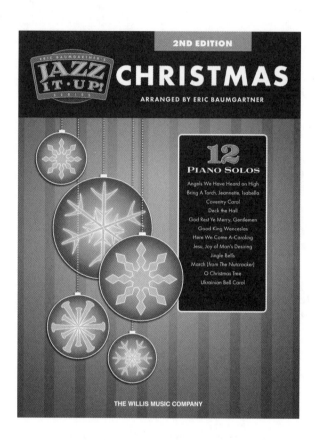

Christmas Piano Solos
HL 00416791
Intermediate to Advanced

Jazz It Up! Christmas, 2nd ed.
HL 00349037
Intermediate to Advanced

Brazilian Sleigh Bells • Christmas Time Is Here • The Christmas Waltz • Frosty the Snow Man • Here Comes Santa Claus (Right down Santa Claus Lane) • It Must Have Been the Mistletoe • Let It Snow! Let It Snow! Let It Snow! • (Everybody's Waitin' For) The Man with the Bag • Rudolph the Red-Nosed Reindeer • We Need a Little Christmas.

Angels We Have Heard on High • Bring a Torch, Jeannette, Isabella • Coventry Carol • Deck the Hall • God Rest Ye Merry, Gentlemen • Good King Wenceslas • Here We Come A-Caroling • Jesu, Joy of Man's Desiring • Jingle Bells • March • O Christmas Tree • Ukrainian Bell Carol.